A HISTORY
OF BREATHING

A
HISTORY
OF
BREATHING
DANIEL MACDONALD

**PLAYWRIGHTS
CANADA PRESS
TORONTO**

A *History of Breathing* © Copyright 2013 by Daniel Macdonald

PLAYWRIGHTS CANADA PRESS
202-269 Richmond St. W., Toronto, ON M5V 1X1
416.703.0013 • info@playwrightscanada.com • www.playwrightscanada.com

For professional or amateur production rights, please contact:
Playwrights Guild of Canada
350-401 Richmond St. W., Toronto, ON M5V 3A8
416.703.0201, info@playwrightsguild.ca

We acknowledge the financial support of the Canada Council for the Arts, the Ontario Arts Council (OAC)—an agency of the Government of Ontario, which last year funded 1,681 individual artists and 1,125 organizations in 216 communities across Ontario for a total of $52.8 million—the Ontario Media Development Corporation, and the Government of Canada through the Canada Book Fund for our publishing activities.

 Canada Council **Conseil des Arts**
for the Arts **du Canada**

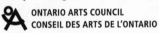 **ONTARIO ARTS COUNCIL**
CONSEIL DES ARTS DE L'ONTARIO

Ontario Media Development Corporation

Cover design & illustration by Patrick Gray
Book design by Blake Sproule

Library and Archives Canada Cataloguing in Publication
Macdonald, Daniel, 1962-. Author
        A history of breathing / Daniel Macdonald.

A play.
Issued in print and electronic formats.
ISBN 978-1-77091-174-1 (pbk.).--ISBN 978-1-77091-175-8 (pdf).--
ISBN 978-1-77091-176-5 (epub)

        I. Title.

PS8575.D6296H57 2013   C812'.6   C2013-904404-3
                                           C2013-904405-1

First edition: August 2013
Printed and bound in Canada by Imprimerie Gauvin, Gatineau

For Averie, my daughter.

FOREWORD

The first time I read A *History of Breathing*, I was sitting at my desk at Native Earth Performing Arts, where I was at the time serving as Artistic Director. By the final few pages I was weeping, swiping tears away to see the words that wavered and bobbed before my eyes, breathing in that huh-huh-huh way you do when you are trying to catch your breath. Staff members tiptoed by my desk, casting concerned looks at each other; I had read hundreds of scripts at my desk and they had never seen me so undone by one.

Daniel's play is a play for the twenty-first century. As the speed of communication increases and events are recorded by bystanders on their phones and uploaded to the Internet, we are witnesses to more and more tragedies and atrocities, and yet still we cannot unravel the meaning of what we're seeing. Why did that young woman kill herself? Why did that man shoot children? Bombing in Boston? In Basra? In Bangalore? The waters rise here and disappear over here. Flood and drought, war and terror, fear and hope. It's the end times, and what's to be done?

Write a play.

Theatre artists have always tried to work things out in the air, on the stage, for themselves, and by extension, for their communities. The Greeks, the Mystery plays, Shakespeare all illuminated for their audiences our relation to kings and gods and asked the big questions—how did we get here, how are we to behave in perilous times, what are our responsibilities to each other? Daniel's play tackles these big questions in the most inclusive of ways, weaving together different cosmologies in an attempt to figure out how we got here, to the edge of the apocalypse, and, more importantly, how we go forward. He tracks backwards through our histories on this planet, our very human failings, our seeming inability to resist war and achieve peace. He shows us how we are all connected, fathers and daughters, fathers and sons, mothers and mother earth, nature and god. And he brings it all together in seven creatures, human and animal, damaged and determined, who together hold the possibility of a new beginning.

"Stories are like breathing," Lily says. Stories *are* like breathing. Our memory and our knowledge are held in our stories, which we tell to teach those who come after about our acts of bravery, or of kindness, about great love, about what we value most. Stories inspire us—they breathe into us the courage to go on.

—Yvette Nolan, July 2013

A *History of Breathing* was originally workshopped and received a staged reading at the Saskatchewan Playwrights Centre's Spring Festival of New Plays, directed by Yvette Nolan, with the following cast:

Lee Boyes
Matt Burgess
Jonelle Gunderson
Simon Moccasin
Curtis Peeteetuce
Danny Knight
Andy Fisher

It was subsequently workshopped and received a staged reading at Native Earth Performing Arts in Toronto, also directed by Yvette Nolan, with the following cast:

Clifford Cardinal
Waawaate Fobister
Craig Lauzon
Richard McMillan
Thomas Olajide
Archer Pechawis
Sabryn Rock

The play was first produced by Persephone Theatre at the Backstage Stage: A Bill & Brett Wilson Project in Saskatoon, Saskatchewan, between November 7 and 18, 2012, featuring the following cast and creative team:

Andrew: Ted Cole
Bobo: Ryan Fiss
Kai: Marcel Stewart
Lily: Stephanie Sy
Muskrat: Curtis Peeteetuce
Toad: Daniel Knight
Turtle/God: Simon Webb

Director/set designer: Del Surjik
Costume designer: Louisa Ferguson
Lighting designer: David Granger
Sound designer: Gilles Zolty
Stage manager: Erin Crowley
Assistant set designer: Jenna Maren
Assistant costume designer: Terri Morgan
Assistant lighting designer: Will Brooks

A NOTE ABOUT CASTING

Because A *History of Breathing* uses archetypal and historical narratives specific to particular cultures and nations, the inclination may be to cast the play with actors specific to these nations/cultures. Creation mythology, however, is universal and ubiquitous. So too is genocide and rape as a weapon of war. I encourage individuals to explore all of the casting possibilities (i.e., "colour-blind casting") that exist within this play as a possible means to further explore the play's themes and questions.

CHARACTERS

Lily—About eighteen
Andrew—Her father
God/Turtle—Played by the same actor
Muskrat
Toad
Kai—About eighteen
Bobo—No more than thirteen, not big or strong-looking—still a child

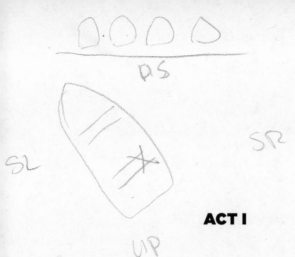

ACT I

Greens, blues, shadows, and ripples.

Sounds of water; the sound of breathing.

From out of the mist and darkness a small boat appears.

In it are TOAD, MUSKRAT, *and* TURTLE.

TOAD is counting the stars. MUSKRAT *is fishing with a stick and string.*

No oar. They just float along.

TOAD   *(looking into the sky and counting)* ...eight hundred and seventeen... eight hundred and eighteen... eight hundred and nineteen... Turtle, what comes after eight hundred and nineteen?

TURTLE   *(eternally patient with* TOAD *throughout)* Eight hundred and twenty.

TOAD   Eight hundred and twenty… eight hundred and twenty-one…
            eight hundred and twenty-two… eight hundred and… Turtle,
            what comes after eight hundred and twenty-two?

TURTLE   Eight hundred and twenty-three.

TOAD   Eight hundred and twenty-three… eight hundred and twen-
            ty-four… eight hundred and twenty… eight…

TURTLE   Five.

TOAD   What?

TURTLE   Eight hundred and twenty-five, Toad.

TOAD   What?

TURTLE   That's what comes after eight hundred and twenty-four.

TOAD   What is?

TURTLE   Five.

TOAD   Five what.

TURTLE   Toad. The number five. That's what comes after the
            number four.

TOAD   Really?

TURTLE   Really.

TOAD   Huh.

TURTLE   We've been through this several times, Toad.

TOAD   Through what?

TURTLE   This conversation.

TOAD   Really?

TURTLE   Really.

TOAD   I have no recollection.

              TOAD *looks at* TURTLE *for a moment.*

              Eight hundred and twenty…

TURTLE   Five.

TOAD   Five… eight hundred and twenty-six… eight hundred and
              twenty-seven… eight hundred and twenty… eight… nine
              hundred.

TURTLE   No.

TOAD   What?

TURTLE   Not nine hundred.

TOAD   What?

TURTLE   It's not nine hundred.

TOAD   Not nine hundred.

TURTLE   No.

TOAD   But it's got a nine in it.

TURTLE   Yes.

TOAD   Would you be able to tell me where the nine comes in the number?

TURTLE   Try to figure it out. What comes after eight?

TOAD   Two.

TURTLE   No. Think higher.

TOAD   Forty-seven.

TURTLE   Lower.

TOAD   Forty-six.

TURTLE   Still lower.

TOAD   Sixty-four.

            Pause.

TURTLE   Think now. After seven comes eight and after eight comes…

TOAD   Dinner.

TURTLE   No. What number?

TOAD   What?

TURTLE   What number comes after eight?

TOAD   (*slightly incredulous*) A *number* comes after eight?

TURTLE   Yes.

TOAD   You're sure?

TURTLE   Yes.

TOAD   Then it can only be nine.

    Pause.

TURTLE   (*a little surprised*) Yes. Good. It… it is nine. Good.

TOAD   Good.

TURTLE   Very good. Continue.

TOAD   Pardon?

TURTLE   Continue. (*looks to the sky*) You know. Counting. You were at eight hundred and twenty-nine.

TOAD   Huh.

    Pause.

(*slowly, lacking confidence*) Eight hundred and twenty-nine… eight hundred and… twenty-ten… eight hundred and eleventy-three…

TURTLE   No…

MUSKRAT   (*losing his mind*) Stop!! Stop it! Both of you!

(*to TURTLE*) What are you doing?? Can't you see he has absolutely no brain for any of this? Every damn night it's the same stupid counting. One… two… what comes after two? Three. Three… four… what comes after four? Five. Every damn night. It's the same cursed game every night and it gets us nowhere.

TURTLE   Muskrat, I'm teaching him his numbers.

MUSKRAT   No! No, Turtle, you're not! You're obviously not because he hasn't learned any of them.

TURTLE   Sure he has, Muskrat. Yesterday he didn't know—

MUSKRAT   Toad. Toad. What number comes after one?

Pause.

What number comes after one, Toad?

TOAD   Uh… two.

MUSKRAT   What comes after two?

TOAD   Uh… two?

MUSKRAT   And what comes after eight?

TOAD   *(more certain)* Two. No. Fourteen. No. Yes. Yes. Fourteen.

MUSKRAT *looks at* TURTLE *to prove his point and picks up his fishing rod.*

MUSKRAT   Now I am trying to fish so we can all have something to eat tonight, and I need to concentrate.

TOAD   You try to fish every night.

MUSKRAT   So?

TOAD   You never catch anything.

MUSKRAT   So?

TOAD   There are no fish.

MUSKRAT   I've seen things swimming.

TOAD   Eels. Houses. Chairs. Boots. No fish. Turtle, there are no fish, right?

TURTLE   I don't know, Toad.

TOAD   I've seen no fish.

well, what have you seen?

           Pause.

           Thank goodness there are stars.
           Turtle, will she come from the stars?

TURTLE   I don't know, Toad.

TOAD   Will it be soon?

TURTLE   I don't know, Toad.

TOAD   How long have we been waiting for her?

MUSKRAT   Forever.

TOAD   Really?

MUSKRAT   About that long.

MUSKRAT *spreads his arms pretty far apart.*

TOAD   That long?

MUSKRAT   Seems like it.

TURTLE   She'll come, Muskrat.

MUSKRAT   What makes you so sure, Turtle? Nothing's the way it was
              supposed to be. There are no fish.

TOAD   That boot this morning was good. There's still some left.

MUSKRAT   But there used to be fish. When we first started waiting. We
              used to eat fish.

TOAD   We did? We used to eat fish?

MUSKRAT   Yes, Toad.

TOAD   I have no recollection.

MUSKRAT   And what about all this water?

TURTLE   It starts with water. Everything starts with water.

TOAD   Is it water then dark or dark then water?

MUSKRAT   This doesn't feel like that water. Doesn't feel like the start.
              It feels like the end.

TOAD   The end? The end of what?

MUSKRAT   If this is the start then why are all those things floating in
              the water? Where did they come from?

TOAD   Maybe they're stars.

MUSKRAT   I think this is the end. I think we missed her.

TURTLE   We haven't missed her. She's how the world starts.

MUSKRAT   Maybe she's how the world ends.

TOAD   Who are we talking about again?

MUSKRAT   The Woman, Toad. The Woman. You were asking about her.

TOAD   Riiiiiight.
Who is she again?

MUSKRAT   Toad! How many times—

TURTLE   Toad. The Woman Who Falls From the Sky. Remember?

TOAD   Yes. No. Yes. Not really. Could you, perhaps, refresh my memory?

TURTLE   Once there was this Woman who was laying beside a tree. In the sky.

TOAD   *(faking it)* Ohhhhhh that Woman!

        Pause.

    Keep going.

TURTLE   And this woman—

TOAD   I love your stories, Turtle. I don't think I could live without your stories.

tap muskrat

Do you like Turtle's stories, Muskrat?

MUSKRAT   (*sincere*) Yes, Toad.

TURTLE   And this Woman looked through a hole beside the tree,
            down through the roots, and saw the sky and the earth…

MUSKRAT   (*helping but trying to move things along*) Covered in water.

TURTLE   All covered in water.
            And she said… What did she say, Toad?

TOAD   (*very unsure, like a child in the first grade*) I'm… hungr…

TURTLE   (*a teacher, helping*) I won…

TOAD   I won…

TURTLE   …der…

TOAD   …der…

TURTLE   …what's… down… there… on…

TOAD   (*suddenly remembering—quickly*) Iwonderwhat'sdownthere-
            onthatearthdownthere!

MUSKRAT   And before she knew it…

TOAD   She found herself falling falling falling through the sky
            down to the earth and some loons came and caught her
            and… and… Turtle, have you seen any loons?

TURTLE   I have not seen any loons.

TOAD   Then what will happen when the Woman comes? Who will catch her and put her on your back, Turtle?

TURTLE   We'll figure something out.

TOAD   Will she drown?

MUSKRAT   She can't drown. She's the Woman.

TOAD   She can hold her breath? Like us?

TURTLE   I don't know, Toad. We'll see.

TOAD   See? I remembered that story.

TURTLE   Yes. That was very good, Toad. Wasn't that good, Muskrat?

MUSKRAT   *(dryly)* Yes. That was very good, Toad. But there is no Woman. No Woman that we've seen, and we've been looking for a long time. For a very long time. It could be that something's happened.

TOAD   Something happened?

MUSKRAT   Could be.

TOAD   What. What could have happened?

MUSKRAT   I don't know. All I know is you're supposed to dive down and bring up earth when she comes, and that's the earth to make the world.

TOAD   I am?

MUSKRAT   Uh-huh.

TOAD   Supposed to dive down?

MUSKRAT   And bring up the earth and put it on Turtle's back with
her and then we take in deep deep breaths and breathe out
onto the earth until it starts to grow bigger and bigger so
it can grow and hold more animals. Don't you know anything, Toad?

TURTLE   Muskrat.

MUSKRAT   Well? He's got to know these things.

TOAD   I do know things. I just forget them.

MUSKRAT   Well you may have to remember them in case you're ever
alone.

TOAD   Why would I ever be alone? That's not how the story goes.
The story has you, me, and Turtle in it. That's the story.

MUSKRAT   It also has the Woman, but she isn't here so maybe something's wrong with the story. Maybe the story has to change.

TOAD   So, this all happens on Turtle's back?

MUSKRAT   Yes. On Turtle's back, Toad.

TOAD   So Turtle holds up the world?

MUSKRAT   Yes, Toad. Turtle holds up the world.

TOAD   Hmm.

> *A pause.* TOAD *looks around.* MUSKRAT *glares at* TOAD.

MUSKRAT　　What, Toad?

TOAD　　Well… if Turtle holds up the world and Turtle's here, then who's holding up the world?

　　　　Pause.

　　　　Who's holding up the world right now?

MUSKRAT　　…Well, no one's holding up the world right now.

TOAD　　No one?

MUSKRAT　　Do I have to explain everything to you, Toad? There's no world to hold up yet. Right, Turtle?

TURTLE　　Right, Muskrat.

MUSKRAT　　It's only water. And how can you hold up water? You can't. You can't hold up water.

TOAD　　Right.

　　　　Pause.

　　　　But something must be holding the water in.
　　　　I mean, you have to hold water in something.
　　　　Right, Muskrat?

　　　　Pause.

MUSKRAT　　Well, of course you have to hold the water in something, Toad. Everybody knows that.

TOAD　　Then what, Muskrat? What's all this water being held in?

MUSKRAT   Toad! I am just about done with all these questions.
           A cup, Toad. All this water is being held in a big cup.

TOAD   A cup.

MUSKRAT   Yes.

TOAD   Aaaaaaaaaaaaaaalll this water.

MUSKRAT   Yes, Toad.

TOAD   So we're floating in a cup of water.

MUSKRAT   Yes, Toad.

TOAD   Then what's holding up the cup?

MUSKRAT   Toad! You are so exprasternating!
           Turtle! Turtle! Tell him what's holding up the cup.

TURTLE   I don't know, Toad.

MUSKRAT   You have to know, Turtle! You're Turtle. You have to know.
           You're the one that's going to hold up the world when the
           Woman comes!

TOAD   What's going to hold up Turtle?

MUSKRAT   Shut up, Toad! Just… be quiet!

TOAD   Maybe that's why there's no fish and no Woman. Maybe
           it's because there's no one holding up the cup. I mean the
           world. I mean the cup. Shouldn't someone be holding some-
           thing up?

MUSKRAT *is getting increasingly concerned.*

MUSKRAT   Turtle?

TURTLE   Hmm?

MUSKRAT   I think maybe we should let Toad dive down and see what he can find. See if maybe he can find some earth, or maybe the Woman already fell and is in the water and we need to bring her up? Maybe?

TOAD   Me? Okay.

    TOAD *starts to get out of the boat.*

TURTLE   No, Toad. Stay. The Woman did not fall in the water.

MUSKRAT   Still. Maybe he should dive down and see if there's earth and that way we'll know that at least there's earth down there for when she comes.

TOAD   Me? Okay.

    TOAD *goes to get out again.*

TURTLE   No, Toad. Stay. She'll come.

MUSKRAT   Well, maybe he should just go see—

TURTLE   Muskrat. She'll come. We'll find earth.

MUSKRAT   I'm hungry.

TURTLE   We're all hungry.

MUSKRAT   We've been waiting since the dawn of time.

TURTLE   That wasn't that long ago.

MUSKRAT   *(spreads his arms wide)* Turtle, it was that long ago. Forever ago.

TURTLE   I'm sure it won't be much longer. Try to fish.

> A *long pause.* MUSKRAT *takes to fishing again and look-*
> *ing in the water.* TURTLE *looks out and sighs.* TOAD *looks*
> *around, bored, wondering, thinking, fidgeting. He looks to*
> TURTLE *then* MUSKRAT *then back to* TURTLE.

TOAD   What do I do now, Turtle?

TURTLE   Count, Toad. Count the stars.

TOAD   Oh. Okay. One... two... Turtle, what... um... what...

TURTLE   Three.

TOAD   Oh. One... two... three... uh... does... uh... anybody know
           what comes after three?

MUSKRAT   She better show up soon, Turtle.

TURTLE   Four, Toad. Four comes after three.

TOAD   Oh. Thank you, Turtle.
           One... two... three... four...

> TURTLE, TOAD, *and* MUSKRAT *disappear.*

> *More water. Shadows. Sounds of whispers. Or breathing?*
> *Crying? It's hard to make out.*

A man appears in the boat. There is an oar but he is not rowing.

Sitting in the boat with a blanket partially covering her is his daughter, LILY, *maybe eighteen.*

They appear to have been at this game for some time. There is only occasional anger in LILY. *Mostly it is resignation, a numbness—a strange, distant humour or irony.*

ANDREW   …Once—

LILY   No.

                Slight pause.

ANDREW   *(very patiently)* Once—

LILY   No. Please.

                He takes a breath and rows and tries again.

ANDREW   Once…

                A pause. LILY *looks up at him. He glances at her. She breathes deeply.*

LILY   …upon.

ANDREW   *(encouraging her)* …a…

LILY   …time.

ANDREW   There. See?

LILY   I need an apple. Do we have any?

ANDREW   You don't need an apple.

LILY   I do. Do we still have any?

ANDREW   We do. In a minute.

LILY   Where are they?

ANDREW   Once—

LILY   I may starve. Would you like me to starve?

ANDREW   No, I would not like you to starve.

LILY   I may.

          A pause. He rows.

ANDREW   Once...

LILY   Your funeral. *(exasperated)* Upon...

ANDREW   ...a...

LILY   ...time...

ANDREW   ...there...

LILY   ...was...

ANDREW   ...a...

          She looks around.

LILY   …ocean.

> *Pause.* ANDREW *looks at her.*

ANDREW   And…

LILY   …this…

ANDREW   …ocean…

LILY   …was…

ANDREW   …a…

LILY   …tired…

ANDREW   …ocean…

> *Another pause.* ANDREW *looks at* LILY.

          …and…

LILY   …the…

ANDREW   …ocean…

LILY   …had…

> *A little longer pause.*

ANDREW   …carried…

LILY   …pirates…

ANDREW   …and…

LILY   …monsters…

ANDREW   …and…

LILY   …corpses…

ANDREW *pauses.* LILY *continues on her own.*

She takes a deep breath.

…and trees and fishes and turtles and boats, and the ocean said one day, "I'm tired, I can't carry anyone anymore." And soon people and things on the ocean could no longer float and everything that went on the ocean would sink to the bottom. But they wouldn't die because the ocean wasn't alive to drown them. So even the fishes who normally can swim in an ocean quite nicely just sank to the bottom and dragged themselves along as best they could all looking for the air to breathe inside the ocean. Until the ocean no longer felt like an ocean at all but a great useless, tideless thing, and it no longer smelled or swelled like an ocean and everything was alive and dead in it at the same time.

Pause. ANDREW *is expecting* LILY *to continue. She does not.*

ANDREW   But then, one day, the ocean got better.

LILY   No it didn't.

ANDREW   It got better and animals—

LILY   *(pleading)* I'm tired. You haven't given me an apple.

ANDREW   Let's finish the story.

LILY   It's finished.

ANDREW   A story about an ocean that's not an ocean is not a story.

LILY   In the little box?

ANDREW   There are only two left.

LILY   One for you and one for me.

ANDREW   They can both be for you.

LILY   What will you have?

ANDREW   There were three. I ate one when you slept.

LILY   Can we eat something other than apples soon?

ANDREW   Tomorrow. I'm sure. He's got to be near here somewhere.

LILY   Does he?

ANDREW   I think.

LILY   You should have asked for directions.

ANDREW   I did. Remember?

LILY   A drowning man clinging to a bloated goat carcass does not count.
He would have told you anything. He probably did.

ANDREW   There was no room.

LILY   I know. And he wouldn't part with his prized goat either.

ANDREW   I've stopped seeing things… people… floating.

LILY   The last thing I saw was that family. Five of them. All face down, like they were trying to see starfish at the bottom. That was two days ago.

ANDREW   Three.

LILY   Did you not run into anyone else while I was asleep?

ANDREW   Do you not think I would have told you had I "run" into someone?

LILY   Then there's only one thing to do.
What I've been asking for the past three days.
What we should have done five days ago.

ANDREW   Five days ago you were still half unconscious.
You writhed in pain and beat the air with your arms.
Was I expected to know what you wanted five days ago?

LILY   We could have still gone back. We still can.

ANDREW   Four days ago we got lost.
Three days ago the sea changed and you finally woke up.
Two days ago was when you started speaking again.
You know what your first words were?

LILY   "I want to die."

ANDREW   Two days ago you woke up and said to your father, "I want to die."

LILY   I do.

ANDREW   You don't.

LILY   If you turn this boat around—

ANDREW   There's no turning this boat around.

LILY   What are you talking about? It's six feet long.

ANDREW   Turn it around to what? To where?
          Oh, yes. Death. To death and starvation.

LILY   Just like here.

ANDREW   No, here is just the slightest bit of hope. Just the slightest.
          Because at least here we're not there.

LILY   You know what Mom used to say?
          She used to say that the only thing worth leaving behind
          are the tears.

ANDREW   I know what she—

LILY   Of regret.

ANDREW   I know what / she used to say.

LILY   But you don't know what it means.

ANDREW   I'm doing what she would want.

LILY   I don't think so. She meant that you can't leave important
          things behind.

ANDREW   She meant that you have to turn away from the past and go
          forward.

LILY   With everything of value.

ANDREW   I have everything of value.

LILY   I'm glad my mother can't hear you say that.

ANDREW   She would agree.

LILY   Everything looks all the same all the time.
             The sea I remember wasn't… wasn't so everywhere.

ANDREW   It wasn't the sea, it was a river.

LILY   I'd like to know how it suddenly became a sea.

ANDREW   You should try to sleep. The sun's long gone.

LILY   I'm amazed it ever bothers to come up at all.

ANDREW   Perhaps we'll find some fish.

LILY   *(chuckles)* There are no fish.

ANDREW   I think I saw some this morning.

LILY   Eels.

ANDREW   Still…

LILY   Monstrous, malevolent, slimy, cruel, sadistic, inedible.
             If you should bring an eel onto this boat I'm leaving.

ANDREW   I saw some birds.

LILY   I keep seeing them too.

ANDREW   You see? They may be tasty. If we could get them to come near—

LILY   Papa. If they come any nearer it's so that *we* can be *their* food.

ANDREW   They're always gone by morning.

LILY   They get closer every day. At night they swim along beside us. I can hear them breathe.
They flap quietly and whisper to each other: "That one's going to be fantastic." Or, "I give her two more days tops." And then they giggle to each other.
They cackle like hens watching the duck get its head snapped off.

ANDREW   I don't think they talk.

LILY   Oh. They talk. They all talk. They talk like the men talked.

          Pause.

          I keep seeing them when I close my eyes. They're like the birds.
It's getting dark. They should be here any minute.

ANDREW   Shh. Lily. Let's do another story.

LILY   It's hard to believe they breathe the same air as we do. They seem so different.

ANDREW   Once...

LILY   But they aren't, are they, Dad?

ANDREW   No. They're just men. Once...

LILY   All we've done since I woke up is tell stories.

ANDREW   Come on, Lily.

LILY   *(sigh)* …upon…

ANDREW   …a…

LILY   …time…

ANDREW   …there…

No response.

…there… was…

LILY   …a…

He thinks.

ANDREW   …little…

LILY   …village…

ANDREW   …and…

LILY   …this…

ANDREW   …village…

LILY   …was…

ANDREW   …a happy…

LILY *looks at him. He cheated.*

LILY   …village…

ANDREW   …with…

LILY   …gardens and trees and small, quaint houses that the happy
            people had made out of everything that the mountain and
            the earth had given them. And the people needed nothing.
            And they would regularly thank the mountain and the earth
            for everything.

ANDREW   See? That's a good—

LILY   Then one day there was a fire.

ANDREW   Lily—

LILY   The fire was started by other people—men and boys—from
            other villages. The villagers didn't understand. And people
            who raced out of their homes from the heat and smoke were
            killed and the people who didn't want to be killed hid out
            in their homes and burned to death and there were screams
            and cries…

ANDREW   That's enough.

LILY   …and humans and animals were calling out for their mom-
            mies and men were…

ANDREW   Lily, stop…

LILY   …men were being herded together and shot or blown up
            or chopped into pieces, and boys too if they had started to
            look like men…

ANDREW   Stop.

LILY   …and to get away people ran into the sea, the massive sea
              that seemed suddenly to be everywhere, and they were
              chased into the sea where they died because they couldn't
              breathe under water, but they couldn't breathe on land
              either because of all the smoke and death, or their lungs
              had been cut out, and the men were dead and the boys
              were dead and the women… the women… the girls and
              the women… the girls… the little girls…

              She slowly stops. There is silence. LILY *is breathing hard,*
              exhausted, but shows little else. ANDREW *looks at her.*

ANDREW   Lily… Lily?

              Pause.

LILY   I'm sorry.
              I know what kind of story you were thinking.
              Those stories are gone. They took them all.

ANDREW   There are still good stories.

LILY   No, Dad. Those are the stories they've left us.
              Besides, there's no one left to tell the stories.
              No brothers, sisters, aunts, uncles, grandparents…

ANDREW   Enough.

LILY   And wives.

ANDREW   Lily. Enough.

              Beat.

LILY   And mothers.

Another pause. ANDREW *looks out into the fading light.*

ANDREW   It won't be much longer. I promise.

LILY   Your promises are making a colossal liar out of you.

ANDREW   I had a map… somewhere.

LILY   We ate it.

ANDREW   Doesn't matter. We'll find him soon.

LILY   Him.

ANDREW   The man with the goat said he saw god.

LILY   He was starving and drowning. Of course he saw god.

ANDREW   Doesn't this seem like a time to find god?

LILY   It seems like a time to abandon god.
Why we're even looking for him is something I cannot fathom.
Unless it's to sleep on solid ground for once.

ANDREW   He's god. Of course he lives on solid ground.

LILY   If he's god why did he make this flood?

ANDREW   Does this not seem like the end to you?
Everything's either burning, dying, or drowning.
It's obvious we're supposed to find god and get help.

LILY   I can't believe *you* got religion.

ANDREW   What do you mean?

LILY   I never heard you talk about god ever in your life. Until now.

ANDREW   / That's not true.

LILY   Except to say goddammit, or oh god, or god almighty, or
                good god, or I don't give a good goddamn, or, to your wife…

                She looks at him, quietly.

                My god you're beautiful.

ANDREW   I'm getting help any way I can.

LILY   From god.

ANDREW   Lily. He's all-powerful. He's… he's supposed to have a lot
                of power.

LILY   Does he have an army?

ANDREW   I don't think / he has an army.

LILY   'Cause if he / has an army…

ANDREW   I don't think he has an army.

LILY   Then what's he going to do for us that you haven't done?
                Turn around and take us back?
                Make it like it never happened?

ANDREW   No.

LILY   Then what's—

ANDREW   You need help, Lily.

LILY scoffs.

Do you want me to lie?
Tell you god will help find her? In one piece?

LILY   She's probably still just lying there.
For five days she's probably just been / laying there on the ground.

ANDREW   By now they've all just been thrown into a pit somewhere.

LILY   By who? Who's left to care enough to throw any of them into a pit?
She's laying there with flies and insects and dogs around her. /
Just lying there.

ANDREW   We're not going back, Lily.

LILY   Then I'm done.
It's where I have to be.
There is no peace until I have found her.
My fate is my mother's.
That is what I wish for.
That is what will happen.

ANDREW   Lily. I did the best I could.

LILY   The best that you could would have been leaving me there.
They were coming back, you know.
They would have finished me off.

Pause. Neither speaks. LILY tries to get comfortable.

I'm not sleeping.

After a moment she's asleep. ANDREW *looks at her, waits a moment.*

ANDREW   *(quietly)* Lily?
Lily?

> ANDREW *adjusts, braces himself, and looks to the heavens in an awkward, uncomfortable solemnity.*

Dear... dear... I mean, oh god. Lord of the... of the universe... If you are god like they say then let us be rescued and brought somewhere where we may get warm and... uh... better.

> *He pauses, thinks.*

No. No. That's not...

> *He breathes and tries again. He prays to the skies.*

Our... father who art... who art...

(to himself) Who art what?

(thinks) Who art the glory of... of... No.

(thinks again) ...

> *The lights fade on* ANDREW. *He prays quietly.*

> *Across the water* TURTLE *appears in his boat.* TOAD *and* MUSKRAT *are asleep.* ~~face back of boat~~

TURTLE   Oh Woman Who Falls From the Sky. Where are you, Woman?

Why are you still not falling? Or are you falling right now and it's just taking a lot longer.

Is it maybe we got lost or the wind blew you somewhere else?

Are you floating on this big sea waiting for us?

Are you swimming under the sea?

Can you breathe water, Woman?

Are you floating on this big sea waiting for us?

Or did you look down at the world through the hole in the earth and become afraid and decide not to fall?

Are we too late? Too early? And where are the fish?

What should we do, Woman? Should we start without you? Should Muskrat and Toad swim to the bottom of the sea and find some earth and bring it back up?…

Oh, Woman, please let this be the beginning and not the end. Because if it's the end then how did we screw up so badly? I am just a lowly animal. And I apologize.

    TURTLE and his boat disappear.

    We come back to ANDREW, *still praying.*

ANDREW   …And if you are god like they say you are, show yourself in your… uh… infinite beauty and magnificence… uh… beauty and…

    LILY awakes in a start as from a bad dream and watches her father as he prays—not completely sure what he is doing in his awkwardness. She watches more intently as she begins to realize.

    …Oh lord of the… universe who brings us everything good.

LILY   What are you doing?

    ANDREW does not stop praying through her words.

Their lines overlap each other.

ANDREW   God is great, god is great… and, uh, the only god worthy
           of praise…

LILY   …Are you praying?

ANDREW   …I praise your holy name, blessed be god, our father who
           art in…

LILY   …Stop that. Stop praying. Right now.

ANDREW   …Our… our father who art… in… who hopefully is…
           …who art, hopefully, everywhere…

LILY   …I'm warning you. I'll get up right now and leap over and
           breathe all that thick, ugly water down into the bottom of
           my lungs. Just to show you.

ANDREW   …in heaven and on earth and everything in between. In
           the seas and the skies and…

LILY   I will. I swear.

           LILY stands up.

ANDREW   …earth. Dear god almighty. You are truly—

LILY   All right then. I'm getting out.

           She does. She gets out. Splash.

           *Everything changes; she is under water and just floats
           there, looking around. It is beautiful, terrible, strange.*

She looks around. It is almost as though she is breathing.

We are immersed in it too, breathing with her. It surrounds us. We are the things in the ocean.

Then...

Her father is dragging her back into the boat by her hair. She is gasping for air.

She resists and fights him off.

This all happens as they are speaking...

ANDREW   Lily! Lily! Come on. Come... That's it, that's it. Back in the boat. Just. Come on. Back in the boat. Lily! Are you crazy? What in the world?... Oh, my Lily. Shhh. Just... It's okay. You can't... Lily...

LILY   Stop! Stop! What, stop! Just stop! Just let me go! Let me go! No! No! Leave me! I'll be fine! I'll... I'll kick you in the head! I'll just kick you. Fuck off! Do you want me to kick you in the head? Let go of my legs! You jerk! I'm not going back in the boat! You can't make me!

   GOD *appears. He is in a small boat, no larger than theirs, with an outboard motor. He is drifting toward them and swearing as he yanks with futility on the rip cord.*

   Perhaps GOD *wears a fishing hat. He looks worn and a little dishevelled, like he's seen better days. He certainly does not look "Godly." There is a fishing net and a fish basket in the boat.*

   LILY *and* ANDREW *stop and stare.*

Oblivious to them, GOD *continues to curse.*

GOD   Either of you have a safety pin?

> *They stare.*

...Paper clip?... Wire?

> *No response.* GOD *yanks at the rip cord a few more times.*

> *A gibberish of swearing ensues. He stops.*

> *The two men look at each other from their respective boats.*

> ANDREW *sees the fishing rod and the other equipment.*

ANDREW   Fishing?

GOD   I was.

ANDREW   Catch anything?

GOD   Sort of. Out for a row?

ANDREW   Um... we... our...

> *Silence.*

GOD   Lost?

ANDREW   Have you seen any land recently?

GOD   Uh... No paper clip?

ANDREW   Do you live around here?

GOD (*looking around a little anxious*) Somewhere.

LILY (*under her breath*) Ha ha. Somewhere. That's funny.

GOD *and* ANDREW *look at her.*

Somewhere. What does that even mean?

ANDREW (*quietly scolding*) Lily.

LILY What. We're supposed to be polite? Perhaps he'll ask us to tea.

GOD I have to get off all this water.

ANDREW Does it end?

GOD Oh god, I hope so.

LILY You don't know? Where did you come from?

GOD How much do you want for that oar?

ANDREW I'm sorry?

GOD You wouldn't have two or anything?

LILY It's not for sale. And we don't need money, we need food. We're starving.

GOD Ah. Everyone seems to be starving.

ANDREW Everyone? There's other people?

GOD Weren't there people where you came from?

ANDREW   Some.

LILY   Many are dead and the living are mostly in hell.

GOD   There is a lot of death these days.
           Did they die in the flood or just die?

ANDREW   Flood?

GOD   Yes.

ANDREW   This is a flood?

GOD   You didn't know?

ANDREW   We fled by water. In this boat we found. We couldn't tell
           when the sea stopped being the sea and became a flood.

GOD   Where did you come from?

ANDREW   From the war. And the fires.

GOD   Which war?

LILY   Pick one.

GOD   And it's just you two?

LILY   (*sarcastic*) Hell no. Can't you see the arc we're towing
           behind us?

ANDREW   Lily.

LILY   Well for fuck's sake. What is he, retarded?

ANDREW   Lily!

LILY   What? This is idiotic. We're on an ocean full of eels.
No whales or fish or turtles or even sharks. Eels.
And the birds that come whisper songs of death in the pitch
darkness.
And a man comes along with a broken motorboat wanting
our oar.
I'm supposed to be polite? I'm supposed to think this isn't
a joke?
Perhaps I'm already dead. Perhaps I drowned in the water.

GOD   Those birds are actually quite good.

LILY   Really. Thank you.

(to ANDREW*)* Can we leave?

GOD   I like the sea. Everything comes from it.

LILY   But nothing's left in it. Nothing good.

GOD   It'll be back. It always comes back.
Things always come back around again.

LILY   Back around.

GOD   Yes.

LILY   And how would you know this?

GOD   They just do.

LILY   Really.

GOD   Yes.

LILY   Well I think this is a sea of death. Or something like it.
           Have you seen all the things floating inside it?
           I have. I just came from there.

ANDREW   We haven't been able to find much food.

GOD   So I might get the oar if I had some food?

ANDREW   Pardon?

GOD   You need food. I need an oar. I have food, you have an oar.

           LILY and ANDREW look at each other. They confer quietly.

ANDREW   Giving up the oar would be suicide.

LILY   Wouldn't giving up food be suicide?

ANDREW   It would probably be our last meal.

LILY   Mmmm. I would love a last meal.

ANDREW   Lily, without the oar, once the food was gone, we would do
           nothing but float around the ocean and then die.

LILY   Oh. You mean like right now?

GOD   I have places to be.

LILY   Well you're not going anywhere without the oar.

           They look at each other across the water for a time.

ANDREW   What kind of food?

LILY   Oh my god, Dad, that's like asking us what kind of oar.

GOD   It'll keep you for quite some time.

LILY   Do you have any idea what giving up the oar will mean?

GOD   I do.

LILY   Oh good. Long as we're clear. I mean it's of no consequence to me but I'd prefer my papa continue to live. Beyond, say, tomorrow.

GOD   This food will keep you for a long time.
Tell you what. I'll paddle away and come back for you after I get the motor fixed.

ANDREW   How long will that be?

GOD   Not long.

LILY   Wait.

> There is a pause. LILY is weighing what she is going to say.

> She looks at her father then back at GOD.

Tell *you* what. We give you the oar and you give us food and when you come back you bring us back home.

GOD   Home?

ANDREW   She doesn't mean that.

GOD   Where's home?

ANDREW   Where the war is.

GOD   Why would you want to go there?

ANDREW   We don't. We're not.

LILY   The oar for a return trip back to where we came from.

ANDREW   If we go back there she will die.

LILY   If I don't go back there I'll die.

GOD   I don't understand.

LILY   So you either turn us around or I am dead by nightfall.

GOD   Is she serious?

LILY   I'm thinking of hanging myself from the bottom of the boat.

ANDREW   She doesn't know what she is saying.

GOD   All right.

        Pause.

LILY   What?

GOD   For that oar I'll take you back.

ANDREW   Sir, you don't—

GOD   I'll paddle home, fix my motor, and then come back and take you back home.

LILY   Sure.

ANDREW   No.

LILY   Yes. Deal.

ANDREW   No. There's nothing to go back to. What's done is done. If it's not flooded over, it's all burned down. There will be no one there.

GOD   I have to be getting back.
What if I take the oar and go and in the meantime you two decide what you want to do.

LILY   Why are you in such a hurry?

GOD   The flood.
My house, my garden may be flooded.

ANDREW   Your garden?

GOD   My garden, my animals…

ANDREW   What kind of animals?—

GOD   *(sigh)* So it's settled. I'll come back for you and take you where you want to go. Now if you'll toss the oar—

LILY   Food.

GOD   Pardon?

LILY   You promised us food. Show us the food.

GOD   Just toss the oar and the food will—

LILY   First show us the food.

> *Reluctantly* GOD *bends down into his basket and lifts up a medium-sized eel.*

              Shit.

ANDREW   Eel?

GOD   Three of these will last you weeks.

LILY   If we don't die from eel poisoning first.

GOD   The taste grows on you.

LILY   I don't want the taste of eel growing on me.

ANDREW   Not a fair exchange.

GOD   You're not really in a position to be negotiating, are you?

LILY   *(right out loud)* Bluff him, Dad.

ANDREW   You will not be getting our oar for any eels.

> *A pause.* GOD *sighs and looks at them. He bends down and picks up two largish fat birds. They have been skinned. They look mostly like small chickens. He holds them up.*

LILY   Chickens?

GOD　　　　Birds.

LILY　　　　Birds. Talking birds.

GOD　　　　They don't talk.

LILY　　　　Oh, they fuckin' talk.

GOD　　　　Two birds for your oar.

　　　　　　　A bit of an overlap…

LILY　　　　…Hasn't anyone heard them talk?

GOD　　　　…They're quite tasty.

LILY　　　　…They've been laughing at me? Encouraging me to kill myself? Things like that?

GOD　　　　Two birds.
　　　　　　It's all I have. There are no fish.

LILY　　　　And a promise to return and bring us home.

　　　　　　　Pause. GOD *looks at* ANDREW.

ANDREW　　Lily…

LILY　　　　And a promise…

GOD　　　　Yes, yes, yes.

　　　　　　　The transaction takes place. GOD *throws them two birds.*

　　　　　　The oar please.

> ANDREW *hesitates. He then reaches out with the oar to hand it to* GOD, *who reaches as well but can't quite reach. They strain some more.*

Wait.

> *Gingerly,* GOD *steps out of his boat and takes a few steps on the water to get the oar. Both* LILY *and* ANDREW *stare, stunned.* GOD *gets the oar and carefully takes the steps back and into his boat.*

ANDREW   How did you do that?

GOD   I have to get going.

> GOD *disappears into the mist and dark.*

ANDREW   *(calling off)* Well, thank you for the food! We'll be here when you come back.

LILY   Or somewhere else.

> *They watch him go.* ANDREW *turns to* LILY.

ANDREW   You see?

LILY   What.

> ANDREW *simply looks at her like she should know what he's talking about.*

(incredulous) You think you prayed him here. You think he's god.

ANDREW   What other possible explan—

LILY   So far all he's done is take our oar and given us a couple of birds to eat.

ANDREW   Lily, doesn't it seem—

LILY   That's the last we'll see of him and without the oar we are now truly doomed.

ANDREW   He promised he'd come back.

LILY   And you think he's going to keep his promise?

ANDREW   I do.

LILY   If he does, it's to take us back home.

>   ANDREW *does not respond.*

Remember?

>   ANDREW *says nothing.*

>   LILY *tries to get comfortable again.*

I'm not sleeping.

>   *She does. They fade into darkness even as we begin to see* TOAD *under water.*

>   TOAD *is swimming and looking, looking and swimming.*

>   *Then suddenly he and we are out of the water and he's climbing back into his boat with* TURTLE *and* MUSKRAT *helping.*

>   TOAD *is breathing heavily and coughing.*

(handwritten margin note: come on back)

MUSKRAT   Well? Toad? Did you find anything? Let me see your hands.

> TOAD *continues to cough and try to find his breath.* MUSKRAT *looks into his hands.*

Nothing? Nothing at all? No dirt?

> TOAD *shakes his head. His breathing is starting to return to normal.*

Let me see your mouth.

> TOAD *opens his mouth and* MUSKRAT *looks into it.*

> TOAD *coughs and spits water in* MUSKRAT's *face.* MUSKRAT *cleans himself off.* TOAD *sits back and tries to recover.*

(handwritten margin notes: get crazy / more chaos / flailing)

Toad. You were down there for about… about…

> *He spreads his arms wide.*

…that long.

> TURTLE *spreads his arms not as wide.*

TURTLE   I think about that long.

TOAD   Felt more like this long.

> TOAD *spreads his arms as wide as he can.*

MUSKRAT   And nothing?

TOAD   Nothing.

TURTLE   Did you see the bottom?

TOAD   There is no bottom.

MUSKRAT   No bottom?

TOAD   No bottom.

MUSKRAT   If there's no bottom then how are we supposed find the dirt?

              No response.

              Turtle? How are we supposed to find the dirt, Turtle?

              No response. MUSKRAT *looks to* TOAD.

              No fish?

TOAD   No.

MUSKRAT   What did you see, Toad?

TOAD   Nothing. I didn't see nothing. There's nothing to see. It's
              too dark.
              There are things floating underneath but I couldn't tell
              what they were.

MUSKRAT   Things. Floating.

TOAD   Yes.

MUSKRAT   Underneath.

TOAD   Yes. Shapes. Dark... shapes. Maybe they were shadows.

MUSKRAT   Things don't float underneath, Toad. They float on top. If
            they float underneath then they're sinking.

TOAD   Nothing was floating on top. They were all floating
            underneath.

MUSKRAT   No. Toad. They were either floating or sinking.

TOAD   These things weren't sinking and they weren't fl—

MUSKRAT   *(losing it)* Toad! They were either floating or sinking! They
            were either floating on top of the water or sinking under-
            neath the water. That's what things do, Toad!

TURTLE   Muskrat. Try to—

MUSKRAT   Who said you should be in this boat, Toad? You've got the
            brains of a bat!

TURTLE   That's enough, Muskrat.

MUSKRAT   Well, I'm hungry. I'm hungry and tired.

            TOAD *holds up a half-chewed boot.* MUSKRAT *slaps it out
            of* TOAD's *hand.*

            I'm tired of eating boot! I can't eat any more boot! Do
            you understand me you stupid toad? I need real food or
            I am going to die. We are all going to die! And if we die,
            the Woman will never start the world because she will fall
            splash into the sea, and because the Woman can't breathe
            under water and can't hold her breath very long, she will
            drown. Is that what you want, Toad? You want the Woman
            to drown?

TOAD   No.

MUSKRAT   Who put you on this boat in the first place, Toad? Who
            decided that you should be on this boat?

TOAD   The story.

blastphemy

MUSKRAT   Well maybe we have to change the story. I'm going to tell
            you what's going to happen here. I am going to dive down
            and find the earth and bring some up and I'll have it ready
            for when the Woman comes. Everybody knows that musk-
            rats can hold their breath waaaaaaaaay longer than toads.
            I don't care if it takes me this long *(spreads arms)* plus this
            long *(spreads arms)* plus thiiiiiiiiiiiiiiiis long! *(stretches them
            even longer)*

            A pause. TOAD *and* TURTLE *just look at him. They are a bit
            taken aback by this outburst.*

            I am. That's what I'm going to do.

            Pause. No response.

            And when I find food, I'm going to eat it all myself.

            No response. MUSKRAT *settles down a bit, looking for sym-
            pathy now.*

            Aren't you guys hungry?

            TURTLE *and* TOAD *nod.*

            Me too. Me too. I'm really hungry.

*give M
the boot*

They sit quietly. They try to get comfortable. MUSKRAT *looks out and down into the water.*

The lights fade on their little boat.

The lights come up on LILY *and* ANDREW *in their boat.* LILY *is still huddled under her blanket but sitting up more.*

ANDREW *looks into the darkness.* LILY *sings a simple song…*

LILY   Speak to me with eyes of green
              And hands as soft as snow
              My ears do see my eyes do hear
              What my heart shall never know

The light broadens to reveal GOD *in his motorboat steering with his now operational outboard motor. There is a rope attached from his boat to theirs and he is towing them along.*

The sound of the tiny motor drones on in the background.

There was a girl who flew the skies
Her shadows were at bay
But now the earth does make her bed
Her bones are made of clay

Tra la la la la la la la
Tra la la la la la lay

My mother was the fairest girl
The earth did ever see
Her bones are falling through the dirt
I'll guard them close to me

Tra la la la la la la la
Tra la la la la lee

Tra la la la la la la la
Tra la la la la lee

The lights and boats begin to fade even as LILY *sings into the darkness, repeating the short chorus.*

The echoes of breathing, rippling shadows, water sounds… these sounds all fade. Silence.

Dry land. A new kind of breathing. Panting. As though someone is out of breath. KAI *appears, seated, eating fruit. A bloody machete sits by his side.* KAI *seems to be speaking off to someone just out of sight.*

KAI The first thing we did was create panic. Panic makes them stop thinking.
You make noise. You use large movements. You wave your machete around.
We didn't even have to speak. We just screamed and yelled.
And I tell you they panicked. Did they ever panic.
When they panicked they started thinking like survival.
This left them with only a few options of escape and we had thought of them before they had so we knew what they were going to do.
We knew what directions they were going to go and who they were going to take.
Mothers rarely leave behind children and so they go slow.
The girls go faster. Unless they have a baby.
We didn't kill them first. We stopped them.
There were about thirty of us. Me and maybe ten more boys and then some men.

We hit at the legs or ankles or shoulders, right at the neck.
They fall quickly.

We killed as many men as we could find and then we took
the boys.

We took the boys and brought them together and then we
put one boy in front of another boy with a machete or a club
and said, "Kill that other boy or I will kill you! Right now!"
We screamed it fast over and over so they didn't have time
to think.

One of us said, "Kill that boy or I will kill your sister. You
see your little sister lying on the ground screaming? Kill that
boy right now or I will chop your little sister in half!" So the
boy killed the other boy. He cried and screamed the whole
time he did it. Once he did that, he would do anything.
They would go anywhere. He'd seen it all. He'd done it all.
He didn't care.

> BOBO *appears. He looks no more than thirteen. He carries
> a handful of fruit, which he sets down. He does not sit. He
> holds a bloody machete.*

Is that your story, Bobo? Is that what they did to you?

> BOBO *looks at* KAI *but does not respond.*

We have to keep moving. See those walls up there? On the
hill? That's where we should go. It'll be away from the water.

> KAI *and* BOBO *disappear.*

> *End of Act I.*

ACT II

There are faint water sounds. That's all.

A light comes up on ANDREW—*alone, isolated.*

This feels like a dream. There is sound, music, something.

ANDREW   Once there was a man who was alone. He was still a young man. But he was always alone. He had no one and almost nothing and most of the time all he did was write stories. And he lived in a small house in a small village by a small mountain. He liked his life because people liked his stories and he would share them and the people would tell each other the stories over and over again, but he wished he wasn't so much alone all the time…

…Then one day when he was out hunting near the bottom of the mountain, he came upon a woman who was lying on the ground. The woman was hurt. She was holding her ankle and crying a little—in the way women cry when they're hurt, *(high-pitched crying)* hmm, hmm, hmm. Very softly. Very much trying not to. And the man said, "Are you hurt?" And the woman nodded. And the man looked up and he saw that they were under a tree and that several of the branches were broken. Very large ones. And he said, "Did you fall?" And she nodded. And he looked up and pointed and said, "Did you fall from there?" And the woman looked up and nodded because she was still crying in that soft way, (*high-pitched*) hmm. Hmm. And the man said, "What were you doing up there?" And the woman just shrugged her shoulders. And then she spoke…

"I was… I was looking down…"

She said, "I was looking down," she said…

"…I was just looking down and then suddenly I was falling."

So the man picked her up in his arms and carried her back to his house. And he took care of the woman and she liked the way he took care of her so much that she fell in love with him and because she was younger and did not have a husband or children yet, she married him. And they lived in the village and gardened and sometimes he hunted.

…And then one day she told him that she was going to have a baby. And that's exactly what she did. And they named their baby Lily. Because she was a girl and she reminded them of the lilies that floated on the pond that fed into the river that was near their village. And the people and the village were very very happy. And everyone grew up together and always had enough to eat and their village was always peaceful. Always.

He turns and looks off at someone we cannot see. He smiles. He fades from our view.

We are on the land.

Water can be heard lapping against the shore.

The land looks like it is a garden. Well, what used to be a garden.

It is completely overgrown with weeds and plants that have overrun everything. It is humid and fetid and full of smells and insects that buzz around.

Occasionally we hear the desperate bleating of sheep in the distance.

The animals' boat is in the water but only TOAD *is in it.* TURTLE *is not there. When the lights come up further we see* MUSKRAT *standing on the shore near the garden.*

TOAD and MUSKRAT *are just looking at each other, a bit in shock.*

MUSKRAT   It is. I swear.

TOAD   Are you sure?

MUSKRAT   Look at me.

            He jumps up and down. He reaches down and picks up some dirt and holds it up and lets it fall to the ground.

            See?

TOAD   I think you should come back, Muskrat.

MUSKRAT   Why?

TOAD   Turtle would want you to come back.

MUSKRAT   Why?

TOAD   I don't think it's ours.

MUSKRAT   Not ours? Of course it's ours. We just couldn't find it before. Now we found it.

TOAD   It's supposed to be at the bottom of the sea. The dirt is supposed to be under—not above. If we find it above what would be the point in having animals that can dive?

MUSKRAT   Maybe the story's wrong.

TOAD   How can the story be wrong?

MUSKRAT   Maybe it's mistaken. Maybe it made a mistake. Stories can make mistakes.

TOAD   What story do you know that made a mistake?

MUSKRAT   Did we find any dirt? Did we find any at the bottom of the sea? No. We did not. There was nothing but dead sea, water everywhere—with nothing. That doesn't sound like the story to me. The story says we find dirt. I found dirt.

TOAD   Muskrat, you're making me nervous.

MUSKRAT   Why? Then, when the Woman comes, there will already be a place for her. We won't have to find a little bitty piece of dirt that we put on Turtle's back and then breathe in and out on it and blow and blow and make it spin until it becomes bigger and bigger and until it's big enough to fit everything on it. That's a lot of work and it would take a long time. A long time. About that long!

MUSKRAT *spreads his arms as wide as he can and holds them open.*

TOAD   It's supposed to take a long time. Making the world takes a long time.

MUSKRAT   How do you know?

TOAD   That's what the story says.

MUSKRAT   All I know is that you dived down to the bottom and found nothing. No dirt, no fish, no bottom. Then I dived down to the bottom, almost drowned and found nothing. No dirt, no bottom. Nothing. Now Turtle's dived down and he's been gone a long time. A really long time.

TOAD   I dove down to the bottom?

MUSKRAT   There is no bottom.

TOAD   When was this?

MUSKRAT   Toad—

TOAD   Were you there when I dove to the bottom?

MUSKRAT   There is no bottom. You found nothing.

TOAD   I have no recollection.

MUSKRAT   I'm going to look around.

TOAD   What if you don't come back?

MUSKRAT   I'll be back.

TOAD   But Turtle's not here.

MUSKRAT   I'm sure he won't be much longer.

TOAD   But we floated away from where he dived.

MUSKRAT   He's a turtle. He'll find us.

TOAD   Don't be long, Muskrat. I don't trust that dirt.

MUSKRAT   I'll be about this long.

He holds his hands open slightly.

TOAD   Try to be about this long.

TOAD holds his hands open even less.

And bring back food if you find some.

MUSKRAT goes. TOAD watches him until he's out of sight.

Bye, Muskrat.

TOAD looks around, pondering what to do alone in the boat.

He and the boat disappear.

Somewhere along that same shore LILY is pulling a rope attached to her boat. The boat is heavy and resists. She is partly crying, partly talking to herself.

ANDREW is sitting near her with a bowl of food, looking around.

He seems calm, amused, amazed at where he is.

LILY   Stop daydreaming and help me with this boat.

ANDREW   Let go of the rope, Lily. It's okay.

LILY continues for a moment, but she's tired. Finally she lets go of the rope.

LILY   He lied. He lied to us. He told us he was going to take us back home and he just took us where he lives. He just took us to *his* home. To his "garden."

ANDREW   Lily. Do you actually think he was going to bring you home?

LILY   Yes! I thought he was going to bring us home. We made a deal with him.

ANDREW   I think he's trying to protect us.

LILY   Protect us? How could he possibly protect us?

ANDREW   Maybe that's what he does. Protect people.
He brings people to his home and protects them.

LILY   Really.

ANDREW   Like his sheep.

LILY   What?

ANDREW   He has sheep.

LILY   So?

ANDREW   Sheep? Flock? His sheep?

LILY   *(realizing)* Oh dear god.

ANDREW   It's true. I saw them. God would have sheep.

LILY   They look half-mad and malnourished.
             They're all running around loose like large, furry rats.

ANDREW   That's his lambs.

     Pause.

     The lambs of—

LILY   Don't even say it.

     A *sheep bleats in the distance.*

     And how can you just sit there? Eating… telling stories…

ANDREW   Lily. He rescues us from a flood. And not just any flood but
             a there's-no-land-anywhere-else-in-the-world flood. He has
             food. He's the only one living.
             He's the only one on land… He has sheep. Lily. He walked
             on water.

LILY   Magic trick.

ANDREW   Miracle.

LILY   I can't believe this.

ANDREW   What if we're the only ones left?

LILY   Then humanity is fucked because our offspring will be born with teeth in their foreheads.

ANDREW   Lily. This is about being alive. We survived. That means something. That means we were supposed to survive. Lily, we were saved.
Look at us! Look where we are! Look what we have here.

LILY   We were not saved.
You were saved. I was… not saved.
No woman was saved. Being alive does not mean you were saved.
It means they took everything else from you and left you with that which now is the most useless. Your life. Because it is not a life.
It is not anything you can do anything with.
I am like that sea. That great flooded sea out there.
I am supposed to have things inside me. Things that one day will live and grow.
I am supposed to be full of… things.

ANDREW   You are alive, Lily.

LILY   Existence is not life! No one just wants to exist.
You can't keep me alive just so that I may exist.

ANDREW   That boat is suicide.

LILY   So?

ANDREW   I won't let you.

LILY   Why not?

ANDREW   I just… can't. You're my daughter.

LILY   That is biology talking! Biology. Nothing more.
            Right now, if it were any other woman whose body had been
            plundered by soldiers, you would turn your back.

ANDREW   I would not.

LILY   You would! You did!
            There were other women fleeing, screaming.
            Did you wrap them in a blanket and hoist them over your
            shoulder and race to the shore? No. You hoisted me. Who
            after a day and a night of men—even boys—parading through,
            taking turns, coming back, while they continued to kill…
            They'd go out and kill and then come back.
            Then they went out and didn't come back anymore.
            A small gift.

ANDREW   I know. A miracle.

LILY   The miracle would have been finding my mother. Alive.
            Whole.
            That would have been a miracle.
            I would have believed in anything then.

            A pause. A sheep bleats. ANDREW *picks up the bowl and gives
            it to* LILY. *She sits against the boat and eats absent-mindedly.*

            A long pause.

            Where were you?

ANDREW   I was talking to god. I was trying to find out—

LILY   Not now. Then.
            When they took me.

Pause.

ANDREW   Hiding. In the woods. Your mother arranged to meet me there.

LILY   Why didn't she?

ANDREW   She went looking for you first.

LILY   At Shala's house.

ANDREW   Yes. But she never got there.

LILY   They killed her. Shala. They wanted to take her but she fought too hard.
She bit some of them—one of them right on the nose, another on the cheek.
She spit his flesh back at him. It was beautiful.
So they got impatient and killed her. Right in her kitchen.
They hit her so many times, they must have killed her twelve times over.
I wanted to live. So I didn't fight as hard. I thought if I begged maybe they wouldn't.

    Pause.

I should have bit their cocks off.

    Another pause. They can't look at each other.

    Pause.

She went looking for me? At Shala's house?

ANDREW   Yes.

LILY   Why?

ANDREW   She refused to go to the woods without you.

LILY   But you went into the woods.

ANDREW   She made the plan, Lily. She told me to.

LILY   Why didn't you say no?
Why didn't you say, "No, you go to the woods. I'll go find her."
Why didn't you say, "I'll find Lily and bring her back to you.
You run and hide and be safe."

ANDREW   She knew what the men would do.
That they would go after the men and kill them first.
She said she would have more time.

LILY   But she didn't.

ANDREW   No. They went after anybody. All at the same time.
They didn't care.

LILY   Why didn't you go looking for her?

ANDREW   I did. I got halfway and they were on her. Some boys.

LILY   Boys.

ANDREW   Yes. Some I knew from other villages. Some I didn't.

LILY   Why didn't you go after them? Chase them?

ANDREW   With what? There were eight or nine of them, all with
weapons.
I had no weapon. So I just watched.

LILY   Why did you have no weapon?

ANDREW   I don't own a weapon.

LILY   There were weapons everywhere. Bats, clubs, machetes.
              Why didn't you—

ANDREW   Your mother forbade it. You know that.
              She knew what happened to men who owned machetes.
              She was afraid I'd use it.
              She was afraid you would use it.

LILY   But to save her.

ANDREW   To save her I would have had to hack eight or nine boys to
              pieces.
              She knew that. She saw me when I ran toward her.
              She looked straight at me and then screamed your name
              to me.
              And then fell. It was very quick, Lily.

              Pause.

LILY   Why didn't you take her?

ANDREW   She was dead. I thought you might still be alive.
              I think that's when I started to pray for the first time.
              I prayed you'd be alive. I think god answered my prayers.

LILY   That would explain why he didn't answer mine.

              Pause.

ANDREW   And I found you.

LILY　　　Tied down to Shala's kitchen table. Covered in her fresh blood.
　　　　　I doubt that was in the prayer.

ANDREW　But you were alive, Lily.
　　　　　And they were gone. So I took you and ran with you to the river.

LILY　　　The river that became a sea.

ANDREW　Yes.

LILY　　　That became an ocean. That became a flood.

　　　　　　GOD *appears. He's holding part of his outboard motor and a dirty rag.*

　　　　　　(to GOD*)* Where are we?

GOD　　　Does that matter?

LILY　　　Yes.

GOD　　　I have some land. Away from the fighting and killings.

LILY　　　And rapes.

　　　　　　Pause.

GOD　　　Yes.

ANDREW　You have walls everywhere.

GOD　　　Protection. Sometimes people climb the walls.

ANDREW   Do they do bad things here?

GOD   No. Nothing bad happens here.
Sometimes they steal. But mostly they're afraid.

ANDREW   Afraid?

GOD   Yes. People are afraid of everything.

LILY   Of you?

GOD   Yes. Even me.

LILY   My father thinks you're god.

GOD looks at ANDREW.

ANDREW   The destruction, the fires, the flood, and then you… walking on water.

GOD   You think I created the flood?

ANDREW   The flood didn't come here.
All your land, your garden, your animals. They're all above water.

GOD   We are higher up. The flood isn't finished yet.

LILY   *(to ANDREW)* Look at him. He's got a garden, some half-starving sheep and a boat with a shitty motor and you're calling him god.

GOD   You wish I were someone else?

LILY   I don't wish anything.

I wish my mother was alive and my father was happy. There.
Can you do that?…

GOD   / No.

LILY   *(not waiting for a response)* …And evil people who raped
           and murdered were dead.
           First tortured and then killed.
           If you're god then you're everything. If you're not then you're
           nothing.
           Can you take care of all that?

GOD   No.

LILY   Then what's the point of you?
           I look at me, my mother. My burning village…

GOD   What makes you think I had anything to do with that?

LILY   I don't. I don't think you had anything to do with it.
           I don't think you have anything to do with anything.

ANDREW   Lily, god's not going to—

LILY   Stop calling him god! He's no more god than you are.
           I am grateful that he found you and brought you here and
           fed you.
           But we made a deal with him and he betrayed us.

GOD   There are things you don't completely understand.

LILY   I'd like to borrow a boat. May I borrow a boat?

GOD   No. We need those boats.
           The water's rising fast.

Many of the trees in the valley are surrounded already.
The sheep are anxious.

LILY   You're going to use our boat to take the sheep?

GOD   I don't know. I don't know what I'm doing yet.

LILY   For god you really don't know a lot, do you?

ANDREW   Lily, he's just doing his—

LILY   Dad! He's taking the boats and leaving us to drown in this fetid garden with the stench of rotting sheep floating around us. This really must be the end of the world.

GOD   There is no end of the world.

ANDREW   Maybe it's the beginning.

GOD   There's no end and no beginning. It just always is.

LILY   Is it.

GOD   I have to go. I have to bring things to higher ground. I could use some help.

GOD takes the boat and drags it off.

Pause.

LILY looks at her father for a time. She stands up.

LILY   So that's it. No boat. No home. No Mom.

Pause.

Okay then.

She starts to walk away with the bowl of food.

ANDREW   Lily.

She turns.

You blame me, don't you?

LILY *can't look at him.*

It's okay.
I have to go help god move things to higher ground.

LILY waits, then exits. ANDREW watches her go, then leaves.

We find KAI sitting with BOBO. The two of them are eating what appears to be sheep flesh. They are tearing at meat.

Scattered about are bits of wool. There are some carrots fresh out of the earth, dirt still on them.

Their machetes are beside them.

KAI   Once when I was about your age? There was this boy.
He lived in a big house on top of a hill with a fence and a swing.
And the boy's swing swung high enough that I would see him appear above the fence any time I went by to the dump.
All the kids' houses on the hill had beautiful fences and animals that were pets that they played with.
And all the kids in the houses up there would swing and appear for a moment above their fences over and over, like things surfacing on the water.

And all I wished was that I could go up and see these kids and play with them and swing on the swing, but I wasn't allowed.

I went to my papa who was a drunk and beat me for amusement. He said I couldn't go to see these boys because these boys were different, and then he smacked me across the back of my head with his belt.

A pause. They are both gorging on food.

But I didn't go away. I said to him, "Papa, why is it that those kids' houses are so beautiful and their yards are so green while I play with bottles and iron rods and pieces of rubber? Why would god do this? Why would he allow this to happen?"

And my father laughed. Like this.

Ha! Ha! Ha! Ha! HaHaHaHaHaHaHaHaHaHaHahahahaha.

"Do you think," he said, "do you think god worries about who got a fairer shake when they came out? Why you, Kai, were born with the devil's finger up your ass while some other boy was licking a silver spoon?

Do you want to live in this tin roof shack the rest of your life?"

And I said no.

"Then you're going to have to do something about it, aren't you?" he said.

"Damn right." I said. "Damn right."

Then he hit me with his belt again.

And I didn't mind it so much this time.

They sit in silence, eating.

So this boy, this boy with the swing had a bike.

And me and my friend P.K.—he's dead now—we wanted it.

So the kid was on the bike, see. Outside his village.

And he was one of the boys who always laughed at us as we walked to the dump.

And me and P.K., we'd always wanted a bike.

At least one that wasn't from the garbage that we didn't have to find a seat for.

Or a wheel, pedals...

Food.

...So we went up to him.

And I'm like, "Hey, nice bike."

And the kid didn't know what hit him.

'Cause while I talked to him on one side, P.K. hit him from the other.

One! Two! Three! Pow! Pow! Pow! Down he went.

And off we went with the bike. It's was a really nice bike. Red. Really really red.

P.K. was on the handlebars.

So that slowed us down a bit and the boy came running and caught up with us.

So we had to hit him again. He went down pretty quick.

So then we kicked him while he was down. Ribs, head. Whatever, you know?

KAI has gotten animated and is standing, demonstrating. He kicks.

Boot! Boot! Boot! Boom.

Pause. KAI is now in full storytelling mode, becoming himself and P.K.

P.K.   Kai?

KAI   What. Boot!

P.K.   Uh… Kai…

KAI   Yeah? Boot! What, P.K.?

P.K.   He's… stop… he's not moving.

    KAI looks to BOBO.

KAI   He wasn't moving.
So we took the bike and got the fuck out of there.
With P.K. on the handlebars.
Now I know what they mean when they say god helps those
who help themselves.

    KAI sits back down. He resumes eating.

    *ANDREW enters, slowly carrying a bushel of corn, and sees
them and stops. He holds his breath, does not move. The
two have not seen him.*

(to BOBO) You have any idea where we are?

    BOBO does not respond but just eats.

    *KAI gets up and sees ANDREW. BOBO turns to look. ANDREW
freezes.*

Hey there, old man.

    Silence from ANDREW, staring.

This your place? You own this place?

    Silence.

The fruit is excellent.

We can see ANDREW *breathing.*

We killed a sheep. Sorry.

ANDREW *remains speechless.*

We came to get away from the water.
It's rising pretty fast, but don't worry. We won't stay long.
We're just catching our breath and then we'll go.

Pause. They wait for a response but none comes.

Sorry about the sheep.
Come on, Bobo.

They exit. ANDREW *watches them go.*

A change of scene. ANDREW *is with* GOD *in another part of the garden.*

GOD *is holding a machete and has a bushel of long stocks of wild-looking vegetation on his back. They are in mid-conversation.*

ANDREW   …But you said—

GOD   I know what I said.

ANDREW   No. I was led to believe—

GOD   You believe what you want to believe.

ANDREW   You make a bargain with us—with Lily—which I was against.

Then you bring us here—which seems like the farthest place from home, and then it turns out that *home* is just outside those walls!
You brought her back to where she wanted to be!

GOD   I said I would and I did.

ANDREW You're not much of a communicator, are you?

GOD   There's nothing to say.

ANDREW But this is the worst place.

GOD   There are far worse places. There is killing and war every-where. Here there is peace and quiet and no wars.

ANDREW I finally believed in you!
It took me forty years.
I thought you might have some answers. I thought you—could save us.

GOD   I did save you.
Is she still alive? Are you safe?

ANDREW But you brought us back home!
You just brought us back to where we were.
This is just part of everything else.
It's not a new world or a new life. It's the same one as before.
I thought this would be paradise.

GOD   I didn't say this was paradise.

ANDREW What are you? A politician? It's what I believed. It's what I was led to believe. You have to take some responsibility for that.

GOD   This is a safe place. No harm—

ANDREW   But I saw some of the men… boys who came into our village.
           What are they doing here?

GOD   It doesn't matter who they are.

ANDREW   They attacked my village. They raped every woman… every
           girl. Lily—
           God. They kill the women by going inside them.
           They don't kill the outside. They kill the inside.
           My daughter is dead from the inside.
           She can barely look at me.

           There is no response from GOD. *He just looks at* ANDREW.

           You have to do something.

GOD   Do? What would you want me to do?

ANDREW   Kill them.

GOD   Kill them?

ANDREW   You can kill them, can't you? You started the flood… /

GOD   For the last time, I didn't—

ANDREW   …you saved us, you have this—

GOD   They won't do anything here. They'll stay for a while, eat
           some of the apples from the orchard, and they'll leave. They
           won't even see you.

ANDREW   They killed a sheep.

Pause.

GOD   They killed a sheep?

ANDREW   And they've seen me.

GOD   Just stay away from them.

ANDREW   What about Lily? If she finds out she'll try to find them and
they'll kill her.

> *In another space LILY appears in dim light.*
>
> *She has a rope with a noose on the end, which appears to
> be fashioned out of sheep's wool, tattered and worn, but
> strong. She looks up.*
>
> *She sees something from which she can hang the rope.
> She hurls the rope upward but it falls back down. She
> tries again…*

GOD   They'll be gone before she sees them.

ANDREW   Won't they stay here because of the flood?

GOD   It's not close enough yet. They'll leave without knowing.
I have to go fix my boat.

> *GOD starts to leave.*

ANDREW   I need one of those.

> *He indicates GOD's machete.*

GOD   Why—

ANDREW   Do you have any more? I need one. To keep us safe.

GOD   You will be completely—

ANDREW   I need one! Where do you keep them?

> *Pause.*

GOD   Behind the barn.

> ANDREW *leaves.* GOD *watches, then disappears.*
>
> *Lights up full now on* LILY *as she continues to try to get the rope to hook onto something above her.*
>
> ANDREW *enters with a machete. He stops and watches her.*
>
> *When she finally thinks she has it fixed, she tugs on it. It falls.*
>
> ANDREW *watches.*
>
> *She emits a sigh/cry of frustration and again hurls the rope upward.*
>
> *It lands again. It seems fixed. She yanks on it. It does not come down.*
>
> *She steps toward it and parts the noose to slip her head inside.*

ANDREW   Lily.

> *She freezes.*

This is not heaven. Not even close.

> LILY *stops breathing. She doesn't move. She doesn't turn.*

> *He stares at the noose.*

It's not paradise either.

LILY   *(softly)* I could have told you that.

ANDREW   We're back home. God brought us back home.

LILY   Back home?
         We're not... we're not somewhere far way?

ANDREW   There is nothing far away.
         It's all the same place.
         The earth, the death, the flood, paradise.
         All the same.

LILY   He just circled around and brought us back? He kept his
         bargain?

> LILY *works her head out of the noose, looks at her father.*

That's a miracle.

> LILY *looks at the noose and then back down to her father.*

Help me.

> *He helps her down.*

He didn't lie to us?

ANDREW *shakes his head.*

He actually brought us back?

ANDREW   He had no choice.

LILY   How far is it?

ANDREW   What?

LILY   Our village. Where my mother is.

ANDREW   You can't go there, Lily.
           Did you look over the walls? There's nothing. Ashes and
           ruins and floods.
           Those same birds are everywhere, just waiting.

           LILY *looks at him a moment. She's not listening.*

           She turns and walks away.

Where are you going?

           LILY *turns back.*

LILY   Do you think he has any more of those?

ANDREW   What?

LILY   Those machetes. I'll need one.

           ANDREW *looks at his machete.*

           A moment as LILY *looks at her father.*

She starts to go.

ANDREW   Lily.

She stops, defiant.

LILY   What. This is what you want, isn't it?
Look at me! I'm alive and I want to keep living!
Isn't that amazing? I'll find my dead mother
and cry over her and wail to the heavens
while I pull out my hair and gouge at my skin
and scream into the earth to take her
and I will lay her deep in the dirt
and laugh at this puny god who can't even start his own
flood.

ANDREW *tries to hold her, to stop her.*

ANDREW   She's gone. You / need to rest.

She's not listening.

LILY   Then with my machete I will kill anyone who had anything
to do / with taking her from me.

ANDREW   The village is gone. / Everything's gone.

LILY   I will hack and chop at anyone—

ANDREW   You will find nothing. / You will find no one—

LILY   Then I will bury the earth / she lay on.

ANDREW   The flood's / taking everyth—

LILY   Let go of me. I am going—

ANDREW   You're tired. You need to lie down / away from all of this.
              Away from—

              He is physically trying to move her. She now fights.

LILY   You can't stop me from killing or dying! You can't physically
              stop me!
              You have to let me go!
              In the boat, on the water. I could hear you hold your breath
              and wait when you hadn't heard me breathe for a while.
              Then when I would finally breathe only then would you
              exhale.
              When I would start to dream, I could feel you beside me.
              Whispering away the terrors while you felt nothing but
              terrors yourself.
              You are trying to be my father. Doing what fathers do, telling
              me stories to chase away the darkness.
              You are so ready to embrace the darkness for me so I won't
              have to.
              But I am not tucked under the blankets at home in bed
              anymore and the darkness is not out there. It's in here.

                  She points to herself.

              You are no longer between me and evil.
              I wish you were.

                  Pause. ANDREW *knows this.*

              Maybe this is my story. Maybe this will be my story.

ANDREW   Lily.

LILY   You were always so brave.
              But now your fear for my life has made you afraid.

              She puts her hand to his face.

              There is nothing you can do about my life. Leave me.

              She kisses him on the cheek.

              I'm going to find god.

              She slowly moves away.

ANDREW   Lily. There's something else.

              She turns back to him.

              There are some people here.

LILY   People? What kind of people?

              Lights. They are both gone.

              MUSKRAT *is crouched down eating a cob of corn quickly
              and quietly. He looks around from time to time like any
              muskrat would and then resumes.*

              BOBO *enters alone with his machete.*

              MUSKRAT *stops, looks up.*

              The two simply stare at each other.

              MUSKRAT's *trying to be friendly.*

MUSKRAT   Are you the Woman?

> BOBO *stands there, unsure of what he's seeing.*

Food. Real food. Over there. On the other side of the garden.

> *Stillness, and then* BOBO *moves toward* MUSKRAT *slowly.*

> MUSKRAT *remains crouched as he approaches, watching.*

> BOBO *simply stands over him.* MUSKRAT *doesn't quite get this.*

> *He holds the corn up to* BOBO.

Would you like some?

> BOBO's *machete slowly begins to rise up.* MUSKRAT *is frozen, holding the corn.*

> *The machete comes down on* MUSKRAT.

> MUSKRAT *is chopped up into little pieces.*

> *They disappear.*

> LILY *re-enters, moving deliberately. She pauses, looks around.*

LILY   *(whispering)* God?... God?

> *She turns and heads in another direction.*

> KAI *enters with his machete and an apple. He cuts pieces off and eats them.*

They both stop short when they see each other.

They look at each other for a time.

LILY's *breath quickens but outwardly she shows little.*

She knows him, his face, his smell.

He does not recognize her. She's pretty.

She is thinking to herself, "Breathe, Lily, breathe."

KAI   Who are you looking for?

She says nothing. Just stares.

She takes a step or two back but KAI *seems uninterested.*

You ever seen a place like this? There's even sheep.

Pause.

Apple?

He extends the apple toward her. She does not move. He eats it, cuts off another piece for himself.

You looking for someone?

No response.

The man who owns all this.

A faint nod. She is looking at his machete.

You coming from the flood?

Another nod.

Did you come to get food? There's so much food. Apple?

He offers again.

LILY *finds enough of her voice.*

LILY   Where did you get that?

KAI   What.

LILY   That machete. Did you get it from… the man?

KAI   No. It's mine.

LILY   I want one. Where can I get one?

KAI   What for?

No response.

What would you need a machete for?

LILY   I'm… I'm going to find my mother.

KAI   Your mother. Where is your mother?

LILY   Here.

Pause.

In the valley.

KAI   The valley.

     LILY nods.

That's where we came from.

LILY   We?

KAI   I have a boy with me. He's under my protection.

     Pause.

Is that your father? The man I saw before?

     LILY nods.

Doesn't he have a machete?

LILY   I want my own.

KAI   Why?

LILY   I'll need it. When I go back.

KAI   Where?

LILY   The valley.

KAI   For what?

LILY   Protection. Like you.

KAI   From who?

     Beat.

LILY   People.

KAI   What people?

LILY   (*losing patience*) I need to go. I need to find my mother.

              She attempts to walk past him.

              He extends his machete. She stops, still a distance away.

KAI   Where is she?

LILY   I told you. In the valley.

KAI   Where in the valley?

LILY   About forty steps from my house lying in a heap of bodies
              hacked to bits rotting in the sun.

KAI   Your mother was killed.

              LILY nods.

              By soldiers?

LILY   (*scoffs a little*) Soldiers? Like your boy?

KAI   He's learning.

LILY   Learning? What's he learning?

KAI   What it's like to be in war.
              That's why I have to leave here.
              I have to find where the war went.
              We have to go back to the war.

LILY   Why?

KAI   That's what soldiers do.

LILY   That's what soldiers do. They go find war.

KAI   Yes.

> *Beat.*

Why go back to your mother if she's dead?

LILY   She needs to be put into the earth.

KAI   Why?

LILY   She was my mother.

KAI   So? Lots of mothers haven't been buried.

LILY   She was my mother. She tried to save me. I'm saving her.

KAI   Save her? From who?

> *Beat.*

LILY   The dogs.

> *She looks hard at him. She has regained some control of her wits.*

Can I have your machete?

KAI   No.

LILY   Why haven't you left here?

KAI   The same reason you haven't. The flood.
              You're not going to find your mother, you know.

LILY   Yes. I am.

KAI   Have you seen out there? The flood came to the valley and
              took everything.

LILY   It doesn't matter. I'm just going to go see—

KAI   There is nothing to see. It's all water.
              There's nothing but water.

LILY   (less sure) I'm… I'm going to go see.
              I was brought back to this place I left.
              It must be to take care of my / mother.

KAI   There's nothing to take care of.
              Go. Go look. Go climb the walls and see for yourself.
              There's nothing. Your mother is gone.
              It's all gone. Washed away. You would have to swim back.
              The water is surrounding / this hill right now.
              Just stay here.

LILY   You have no idea what you're / talking about.

KAI   Why do you think I'm still here?
              Do you think I want to be stuck here?
              What is there to do here? Eat? Kill sheep?
              How can I be a soldier here?
              I have to get back to the war.
              I'm going to get some directions and a boat, and me and my
              boy will go back to the war where we can do some good.

Your mother is gone like all the other mothers.
No machete in the world will help you find your stupid mother.
They killed her, the birds ate her, and the flood took what's left of her away.

LILY stands there motionless, almost out of breath.

She knows this. She has known this all along.

She turns, looks out as though beyond the garden to the valley, then pauses and turns back to face KAI again.

She looks at him, then at his machete, and takes a deep breath.

She looks straight at him. KAI has taken another slice of apple.

LILY   You mean your boy killed her.

KAI   *(nonchalant)* Fine. My boy killed your mother.

LILY   And what were you doing while little boys were killing their mothers?

KAI shrugs.

You don't recognize me, do you?

KAI   No.

LILY   You've never seen me.

KAI   No.

LILY   You're from the village beside mine.

KAI   So?

LILY   So? What did you do to the village by the mountain that
              was beside yours?

KAI   We did what had to be done.

LILY   And what was that?

KAI   They had to be eliminated.
              Our land had to be purified.

LILY   Purified? Of what?

              KAI *looks at her.*

KAI   I know what you are.

LILY   Yes. I'm sure you do.
              You've seen a thousand like me.

KAI   You're one of those.

LILY   And you are one of those.

KAI   You got away.

LILY   Apparently not.

KAI   Where did we get you?

LILY   My friend's house.

KAI　　Did we get her?

LILY　　No. You had to kill her. She fought like an animal.

KAI　　It happens.

LILY　　Then you tied my arms to the kitchen table.

　　　　*LILY clasps her wrists together and raises her arms above
　　　　her head.*

　　　　This ring any bells?

KAI　　Hard to say. It wouldn't be the first time we tied a girl to the
　　　　kitchen table.

LILY　　It took four of you to hold me down.

KAI　　Four? Not bad.

LILY　　I remember which one you were.

　　　　He laughs.

KAI　　How could you—

LILY　　Ninth. You were ninth. Eight other men before you.
　　　　Easily eight more after. I lost count.
　　　　You were early enough that I had not yet passed out.
　　　　You put your hand over my mouth and face. My nose was so
　　　　bloody I could barely breathe. I tried to will myself to die.

　　　　LILY lowers her arms.

After a while someone would slap me awake and you would
start all over.
Then you would go out and kill for a while and then come
back again.
Each of you had your own smell, your own sound,
your own way of breathing and grunting.
I'd know you even if you chopped my head off.

KAI   We don't often do that to the women.

LILY   No. You let us live. You want us to live.

KAI   This way no one will want you. No man will have you.
You're finished. We take you, we take everything.

LILY   *(an inward smile)* This must be it.

KAI   What?

LILY   Why he brought me here.

KAI   Who?

LILY   God. We have been brought back together, boy. It must be
for this.

KAI   For what?

LILY   My mother's gone. The village is gone. The valley's gone.
Everything's gone.
But you are here. In front of me. With your machete.

And I am here.

KAI   So?

LILY   Doesn't this mean anything to you?

KAI   Like what?

LILY   Look at you. One silly, broken girl and you can't even kill her.

KAI   I already did.

LILY   Not quite.

KAI   So what now? You want me to finish you off?

LILY   Maybe I'll finish *you* off.

KAI   Me?

LILY   Maybe we get to see what death really feels like. Like my friend Shala? Like my mother?

KAI   How are you going to show me that?

LILY   I'll come over there and take your machete and break you with it.

KAI   (*amused*) You. You're going to come here and kill me with my own machete?

LILY   Or leap at you and tear your eyes out.

KAI   (*laughing*) I'd like to see you try it.

LILY   Or bite out a piece of you and spit it in your face.

KAI   Come on. Come. Come and try. You know what's more likely?

LILY   That I'll die trying?

KAI   Much more likely. Come on then. Come here and get my
            machete.
            Come here and try to kill me.

> LILY *thinks, watches. Her breath quickens.*

> KAI *brandishes his machete.*

            Come on. Come and get it.
            You really want to die?

LILY   I've tried. Believe me.
            But Death doesn't want me. He keeps spitting me back up,
            taunting me with promises he doesn't keep.
            Maybe this will be the exception.
            Is that what keeps happening to you, boy?

KAI   I'm alive. I'm going to stay alive.

LILY   To do what you have done you must be dead a million
            times over.

KAI   Are you coming to get the machete or not?
            I have a war to go to. Hurry up.

> LILY *stands there breathing and looking at him and the
> machete.*

> KAI *tosses the machete to her feet.*

            There. How about that?
            Come on. I don't have all day.
            I have to go find a boat and the boy and the war.

LILY stares down at it.

Take it.
You want to find out what death is really like? Then let's
find out.

LILY still stares.

KAI decides.

*He walks over to her, grabs her by the back of the neck, and
pushes her down so that she's kneeling over the machete.*

He stands over her.

Pick it up.
You want to kill me? Do it.

He holds her down. She doesn't move.

*KAI gets down on his knees and picks up the machete and
forces it into LILY's hand and closes her hand around it.
She does not look at him.*

How does it feel?

He's kneeling in front of her now.

Can you do it? Come on.
The first time is the hardest. It's much easier after that.
After what's been done to you, you should be ready to kill
or die.
Just like us.

He waits.

She kneels up and looks at him, weakly holding the machete by her side.

See? I told you. You're nothing. There's nothing left of you.
Dead people can't kill.
I am going to get a boat and I am going to leave this place
and I am going to find the war while you rot here from the
inside!

She looks at him for another moment.

She breathes and gets up, holding the machete to her side.

She stands above him as he continues to kneel.

LILY   Kill you? Look at you.
Go. Go, go find your war. It's all you are.

She begins to walk away then remembers and drops the machete to the ground.

I have to find my father. He thinks he's supposed to kill you.

She starts to exit. KAI yells after her.

KAI   You see? You can't even try.
You could have killed me. I might have even let you!
But you're too weak, too dead to try. There's nothing left
of you!
That is what victory looks like!

KAI is on his knees, alone, looking off after her.

ANDREW appears from behind, out of the darkness.

He is slowly raising his machete.

KAI mumbles to himself as he crawls toward his machete.

I am going to find a boat and I am going to get on the water and I am going to find my war and my boy and we're… we're…

He hears a noise and turns without a machete in his hands.

ANDREW appears from behind KAI. He looks like a different person. He breathes heavily. KAI turns and sees him. ANDREW moves in on him and raises his machete.

They disappear…

Colours and light from water return. The water is rising.

We can see the speckles and shadows. We can hear it now.

We see TOAD. He is walking quietly on land. His slightly webbed feet are leaving small puddles of water. He is talking in half-whispers.

TOAD   Muskrat?… Muskrat?…

BOBO enters running, out of breath, with his machete.

He is holding a piece of MUSKRAT's pelt.

It still has flesh and blood attached.

His feet leave a trail of water and blood.

TOAD enters opposite. They stop and stare at each other.

Hello. Have you seen Muskrat?

No response from BOBO.

Are you the Woman?

BOBO *just stares, out of breath, confused. He has somewhere to go.*

Have you seen Muskrat?

Again, BOBO *does nothing.*

TOAD, *puzzled, slowly wanders off.*

BOBO *watches him for a moment and then looks down at the
muskrat pelt in his hand and runs off in the other direction.*

ANDREW *reappears holding a bloody machete.*

He is standing over KAI's *hacked body, breathing heavily,
crying, snot and blood dripping from him.*

He lowers himself before the body.

He drops the machete. He kneels, exhausted.

BOBO *enters quickly, looking for* KAI *and holding the pelt.*

ANDREW's *back is to* BOBO. *He doesn't hear him.*

BOBO *stands and stares at him for a moment and sees* KAI's
dead body.

He steps quietly toward ANDREW, *machete raised.*

Darkness.

The darkness is overtaken by the sounds of water, and the entire space seems to fill with it, speckled light appearing everywhere.

The light reveals LILY. *She sits over her father's destroyed body.*

She is not crying. But she is only partly there. She is looking at her father like a god would look down toward earth at the sad events below her.

TOAD *enters. He sees* LILY. *He keeps his distance.*

He looks at her and at ANDREW's *body. He whispers.*

Have you seen Muskrat?

LILY *does not respond. She doesn't move.*

Are you the Woman?

LILY *looks up at him from where she sits.*

Where did you come from?

LILY   Here.

TOAD   Did you fall?

A pause. She thinks about this.

She nods.

We've been looking for you for a long time. Probably this long.

TOAD spreads his arms out.

LILY   Is that a long time?

TOAD   Where I come from, that's a very long time.

LILY   Where do you come from?

> *A pause. TOAD has no idea how to answer this. He does his best.*

TOAD   A boat.

> *Pause. TOAD is not sure what to do next.*

So… you're the Woman.

> *LILY hesitates, then nods.*

We should leave then. We have things to do.

> *TOAD stoops down and picks LILY up in his arms. But she stops him. He stands there for a moment. He sees ANDREW's torn body. He's not sure what to make of it. LILY looks down at the remains of her father.*

LILY   I have to bury my father first. I have to put him in the ground. I never buried my mother. I have to bury my father.

TOAD   I don't think I ever had a father.

LILY   They fight the darkness for their daughters.
         They'll do anything.

> *They are gone.*

Somewhere else GOD *appears. He has his outboard motor and is tinkering with it with a tool. A machete lies by his side.*

BOBO enters with his machete and the bit of muskrat pelt.

He sees GOD *and stands there.*

GOD *finally turns and notices him.*

For a moment GOD *freezes and picks up the machete.*

They stand there and look at each other. BOBO *tosses the* MUSKRAT *pelt to the ground at* GOD's *feet.*

GOD   For me?

No response. Not even a blink from BOBO.

God picks up the pelt and holds it.

It's soft. Thank you. Is there more?

No response. BOBO *looks down.*

The flood is coming. I'll have to leave.
Do you have anywhere you can go?

BOBO simply looks at him. Finally he shakes his head.

You should come with me on my boat.
Come. I'll find you some food.

They go.

That world disappears.

Then... water.

Greens, blues, shadows, and ripples appear.

Something is different. Newer.

From out of the darkness, a small rowboat.

In it are TOAD *and* LILY.

TOAD *is looking into the sky and counting.*

TOAD ...eight hundred and seventeen... eight hundred and eigh-teen... eight hundred and nineteen... Woman, what comes after eight hundred and nineteen?

LILY Eight hundred and twenty.

TOAD Eight hundred and twenty... eight hundred and twenty-one... eight hundred and twenty-two... eight hundred and... Woman, what comes after eight hundred and twenty-two?

LILY Three.

TOAD Eight hundred and twenty-two...

He hesitates, looks at her.

...three... four... five...

LILY No, Toad. Twenty-three.

TOAD What?

LILY   Eight hundred and twenty-three.

TOAD   Eight hundred and twenty-three what?

LILY   It's not important, Toad.

> TOAD *looks up at the stars*

TOAD   Is that where you came from, Woman?

> LILY *looks up.*

LILY   Yes, that's where I came from. The stars. We all came from
            the stars.

TOAD   We all came from the stars?

LILY   Yes.

TOAD   I have no recollection.

LILY   Neither do I.

TOAD   Long ago?

LILY   Very long.

TOAD   That long?

> TOAD *spreads his arms out.*

LILY   Longer.

TOAD   That long?

LILY   Much much longer.

TOAD   I need Turtle here to explain to me how long that is.

LILY   Turtle?

TOAD   Turtle. He was with us in the boat.

LILY   Where is Turtle?

TOAD   He dove down to the bottom to find you but he never came back.

LILY   Oh. I'm sorry.

TOAD   No. I think he stayed down so he could hold up the world.

LILY   Hold up the world?

TOAD   Someone has to hold up the world. Nobody was holding it up.

LILY   Oh. That must have been bad.

TOAD   It was bad. There were no fish.

LILY   And now there's fish?

TOAD   I think so. I think I've started to see fish.

LILY   All because Turtle is holding up the world?

TOAD   All because Turtle is holding up the world.
          He's holding up the world that the sea is on.

He's perfect to hold up the world. He has a big back.
Soon I'll have to dive down and find some earth to put you on.

LILY You can hold your breath long?

TOAD Very long. I can hold my breath this long

He holds his arms out again.

How long can you hold your breath?

LILY About this long?

She holds her fingers pretty close together.

I'm supposed to breathe air.

TOAD I'm supposed to breathe air too.
But it doesn't really bother me that much when I can't.
But I'm not a fish. So I have to come back. Fish breathe water.

LILY If I breathed water I'd drown.

TOAD And that's why you're not the one who is supposed to dive
down to find some earth.

LILY How do you know about all this?

TOAD I don't know. I just know.

LILY You know lots of things, Toad.

TOAD I don't really know things. I just remember them.

LILY Then you remember lots of things.

TOAD   I only remember the story.

              Pause.

LILY   Story? You know a story?

              TOAD nods.

              Can you tell me the story?

              TOAD takes a deep breath.

              His shoulders heave.

              He braces himself.

              This is a lot to ask of him.

TOAD   Okay. But you should know the story is never the same twice.
              When the story started, there was me and Turtle and Muskrat.
              Now there's me and the Woman.

LILY   The story always changes?

TOAD   It always does. But it stays the same too.
              It always starts with flood.

LILY   I thought it ended with flood.

TOAD   Start. End. All the same.

LILY   Stories… stories are like breathing.

              He takes a deep breath.

TOAD   Once there was this woman who was laying beside a tree.
In the sky.
And she looked through a hole beside the tree.
Down through the roots, and saw the sky and the earth.
Covered in water.

> *The lights are beginning to fade. The ripples of water are getting brighter, speckling everything. It's beautiful.*

LILY   And what did she say?

TOAD   She said, "I'm hungry."
No. No. Wait. She… she said, "I wonder what's down there on that earth down there."

LILY   And?…

TOAD   And before she knew it…
She found herself falling falling falling falling falling through the sky down to the earth…

> *The lights fade. The water ripples.*

> TOAD *continues the story into the fading light.*

> LILY, TOAD, *and the boat disappear into the darkness.*

> *The end.*

ACKNOWLEDGEMENTS

Ivan, Averie, Del Surjik, Yvette Nolan, Colleen Murphy, Mary Blackstone, Johanna Bundon, Judy Wensel, Jonelle Gunderson, Sabryn Rock, Melanie Rogowski, Aboriginal Playwrights Circle, Jamie Lee Shebelski, Wes Pearce, Kathryn Bracht, Brian Bowley, Heather Inglis, Kenn McLeod, Michael Scholar Jr., the Saskatchewan Playwrights Centre, Mark Claxton, Gordon Portman, Pam Halstead, Jayden Pfeiffer, Will Brooks, Gilles Zolty, Cavan Cunningham, the Enbridge playRites Awards, Alberta Theatre Projects, Native Earth Performing Arts, and Persephone Theatre.

Daniel's plays include *Pageant, MacGregor's Hard Ice Cream and Gas, Velocity, Johnny Zed! The Musical!*, and *Radiant Boy*. He has also collaborated with students on several full-length plays for high schools (*Flock Formations, Tragedie*, and *Waking*). His plays have been produced and workshopped across Canada and the US. He is a two-time recipient of the City of Regina Writing Award and a recipient of the Enbridge playRites Award for Established Canadian Playwright. He also has an M.Ed. and an M.F.A. in directing. Recently he devised a new work with students for the Edinburgh Festival Fringe in Scotland.

transformational
   birth - death - rebirth
Start in water → go to land
new beginnings
fertility

   Kohlburgs
→ Levels of moral reasoning

---

volumn
more endearing polk
leave boot and fishing rod